MW00975795

Choose
Your Daily Decisions
Determine Your Destiny

Steve Kelly

Copyright © Wave Church, Inc. & Wave Publishing LLC, 2014.

All rights reserved. No portion of this book may be reproduced, stored in a retrieval system, or transmitted in any form or by any means, without the prior written permission of the publisher.

Table of Contents

It's Your Choice

From the moment you peel your eyes open to face another day until you dive into bed for the night, every day of your life is a never-ending succession of decisions.

Do you hit the snooze button when that annoying alarm rings and vibrates beside the bed?

Do you wear the white shirt or the blue shirt? The brown dress or the black and white pantsuit? Heels or flats? Paper or plastic?

Each minute, every hour, brings an endless series of choices that must be made in order to progress through the day. Many of these selections are subconscious. You "choose" to turn left at the end of the street out of your neighborhood. But, to go the other direction would be out of the way, so it's a choice only by the strictest definition.

Other decisions are firmly and tangibly engaged by our conscious mind. Do I feel like tacos or pizza for lunch? Am I going to exercise this week? Will I ask my co-worker to stop playing his music so loudly?

These examples are common to everyone. We routinely experience the mundane but necessary options that define the periphery of daily life. In the end, however, we must make choices. Otherwise, we wouldn't really have a functioning life. We would just be breathing, and that would not only become very boring, it would ultimately end your need to choose. Even *not choosing is a choice.*

The simple and familiar regular decisions are not very difficult. Sometimes annoying, but rarely consequential. Which is why they are relatively easy. When the consequences are insignificant, it's not challenging to choose.

What about when a decision has meaningful and widespread implications? What about a choice that will reverberate for several generations and perhaps beyond?

These life-altering decisions are weighty and often involve deep thought and planning. Some of the most common decisions that people make are who to marry, whether to buy a house, or the ultimate life-altering decision: having children.

While all of these decisions are important, their significance withers like a morning mushroom in the blazing summer sun when compared to the ultimate choice every human must make. The decision that transcends all others is the response to the question: "What do you make of Jesus Christ?"

This decision is foundational to every other decision you make. Is Jesus Christ God incarnate, as He declared to the world nearly 2000 years ago? Is He the Son of God sent to redeem man from the curse and give us the promise of eternal life? Or was He just a "good man", a "philosopher" who made some idealistic comments about loving your neighbor and turning the other cheek?

Everyone has to make a decision about Jesus. Even Pilate, the Roman leader, was forced to ask the question, as he did to the Jewish leaders: "What shall I do with this man, Jesus?"[1]

Everyone has an opinion about Jesus. His name is unlike any other on Earth. It heals the broken; it rescues the lost. It divides friends; it unites enemies. Make no mistake, when it comes to Jesus Christ, you must choose. Lest you think you don't have to engage this topic, remember; ***ignoring Him is still making a choice.***

Whatever people may think or say about Jesus, He was anything but ordinary. The incredible legacy He left is another compelling reason to believe Jesus *is* the Son of God. As the secular historian Will Durant famously wrote:

That a few simple men should in one generation have invented so powerful and appealing a personality, so lofty an ethic and so inspiring a vision of human brotherhood, would be a miracle far more incredible than any recorded in the Gospels. After two centuries of Higher Criticism the outlines of the life, character and teachings of Christ, remain reasonably clear, and <u>constitute the most fascinating feature in the history of Western man</u>.[2]

Everyone must choose what he or she will do about Jesus. The singular mission of Wave Church is to help people make the right choice about Jesus. Wave Church exists to help people choose to accept Him as their Lord and Savior. The Bible teaches that Heaven rejoices over one person who comes to Jesus and repents.[3] I often say my sole reason for being is to give Heaven a reason to party. That is why the main ambition of Wave Church is for more people to receive Jesus.

God sent Jesus to rescue us from our sins. God loves us so much He gave Jesus, His only Son, to save our souls and give us a purpose for life on this earth and an explanation for life after earth.

As John 3:17-18 explains, "For God did not send His Son into the world to condemn the world but that the world through Him might be saved. He who believes in Him is not condemned; but he who does not believe is condemned already, because he has not believed in the name of the only begotten Son of God."

If you haven't yet made a choice about Jesus, I urge you to do so. Don't wait any longer. Discover the truth and power of God's plan for your life. Enter the mysterious, overwhelming, all-redeeming love of Jesus. It's not hard. All you have to do is call upon His name. Ask Him to forgive your sins and accept Him into your life. Surrender your will to His and begin the uncovering of His desire and design for your future.

How does a person accept Jesus? It's as simple as asking Him. The Bible explains it in two easy steps:

1. Confess with your mouth
2. Believe in your heart

Don't take my word for it, however. Here's what Romans 10:9-10 says:

"If you confess with your mouth the Lord Jesus and believe in your heart that God has raised Him from the dead, you will be saved. For with the heart one believes unto righteousness, and with the mouth confession is made unto salvation."

That's it. Confess and believe.

If you've never done this before, contact us via www.wavechurch.com. We'll do everything you let us do to help you with this choice. We'll help you move on to life in Christ and guide you in the next choice – living for Him.

Long before Jesus came to Earth, man was given the opportunity and the power to choose. From the very beginning, literally, God made a choice that influenced every single human being. As He created us, He made a dramatic decision – He decided to give us a choice. He didn't want the pinnacle of His creation – mankind – to be robotic, slavish beings. No, He loved us so much that He allowed us to select Him in return. Or reject Him. God won't force Himself upon anyone, as demonstrated in the earliest days after the dawn of Creation.

As early as the second chapter of Genesis, the first book of the Bible, people chose. Would they obey the One who created them, or would they listen to the deception of Satan?

Adam and Eve were fooled by Satan, and chose contrary to God's commands. As a result, they were banished from the Garden of Eden and were left to toil and struggle on the Earth. From that day to this, every person born on this Earth has been faced with the same dilemma.

In Deuteronomy 30, God introduces His people, in no uncertain terms, to the extraordinary implications of man's free will and God's omnipotence. The following is an adaptation of that chapter:

(v.1-10) *I, the Lord your God, have set a blessing and a curse before you. When you return to Me, I will bring you to the land that your fathers possessed. I will prosper you and multiply you more than your fathers. I will curse your enemies and you will obey My voice. I will make you abound in all your work. I will again rejoice over you, if you obey My voice, and if you turn to Me with all your heart and soul.*

(v.11-20) *For My commandment is not too mysterious for you. It is not beyond your reach. It is very near you, it is in your heart. You can do it. See, I have set before you today life and death, good and evil. If you obey Me, you will live and prosper. If you turn to other gods, you will surely perish. I have set before you the CHOICE of life or death; please choose life, that both you and your family to come may flourish. Love Me and obey Me, for I am your life. Choose ME.*

In this passage, God reveals to the Israelites the power and consequence of the ultimate choice. They were given the same opportunity each of us is given today. They could choose to follow and obey God and therefore, choose life and blessing for themselves and their descendants.

Their decision was between life and death, and God allowed them the chance to make the right choice. Now, each of us must also make that choice.

Life or death? Which will you choose?

Choose God; that you might live and prosper.

Remember all those options mentioned at the beginning of this book? You know, what to wear and eat? Who to marry, etc.?

Well, if you make the right choice on this foundational decision – following God – you will be led and enabled to make the right choice in every other area of your life. And, since God has given us the option of choosing or rejecting

Him, once we've chosen Him, He also gives us the option of making choices in how we pursue God's will for our lives. More on that later.

It's wonderful to cement the decision to accept Jesus and to follow God. Without that decision, all the rest of our decisions are next to meaningless. Having made that decision, however, we still wrestle with the classic question that Chuck Colson used as a book title in 2000:

How Now Shall We Live?

Great question. How should we live? How do we choose? How can we know we are making the right decisions? The *best* decisions?

God has given us the answer. He may have given us free will, but He didn't give us free reign. He is still King of all Creation, and He freely shares His wisdom through His Word and His Spirit. He came to help you make the right decisions. You can choose life.

Now is your time to ***CHOOSE: Determine Your Destiny through Your Daily Decisions.***

Renew Your Mind

Information is critical to any decision. Typically, the more informed a person is on a matter, the better his or her decision will be regarding it. We process information and gain understanding through the activity of our mind. Within the intellect of man, logic and reasoning occur.

For example, without the ability to internalize and conceptualize details of engineering and science, we wouldn't have suspension bridges that enable us to travel across deep canyons and broad rivers. Without an understanding of the function of oxygen and carbon dioxide, we wouldn't be able to dive beneath the ocean's surface for extended periods, or travel to outer space.

The activity of the mind is the cornerstone of human decision-making. With this in mind, the starting point for determining how to make choices as God desires is by understanding how to *renew your mind.*

The Mind of Christ

If you are a Christian, then Christ is in your heart. Now, let Him into your mind. Or rather, replace your mind with His. A recent popular trend in Christianity was the idea "What Would Jesus Do?" This WWJD theme was promoted through bracelets, T-shirts, etc. It was an attempt to inspire Christians to behave as Jesus did.

For this chapter, I encourage you to consider the value of WWJT? What Would Jesus Think? You must first adopt the mind of Christ before you can behave like Christ. It's not enough to "do" like Jesus. **We must *think* like Jesus.**

Philippians 2:5 encourages us to, "Let this mind be in you, which was also in Christ Jesus."

What does that mean? We can't get a brain transplant with Jesus, can we? What, exactly, did Paul mean when he told the people at Philippi to "have the mind of Christ"?

A great place to begin understanding this is to continue reading the verses that follow Paul's encouragement. In Philippians 2:6-11, we read a clear explanation of Jesus' behavior, which demonstrates that His mind enables us to follow His example.

Be Humble

"Though Jesus was in the form of God…He made Himself of no reputation. He *humbled* Himself and took on the likeness of men…He *humbled* Himself and became obedient to the point of death, even death on the cross.

Therefore, God has highly exalted Him and given Him the name above every other name, that at the name of Jesus every knee should bow…and every tongue should confess that Jesus is Lord, to the glory of God."[4]

Paul describes the mind of Christ through the actions of self-sacrifice that Jesus did for all of humanity. The actions that led Him to die on the cross were rooted in an attribute that is all too rare among men, *humility*.

The first step in having the mind of Christ, and thus in renewing your mind, is the step of humility. This makes sense in both the spiritual and logical realm. In order to learn, to receive and believe information, theory or concept, you must first be humble enough to accept that there are things you don't know.

Humility is an ancient virtue that requires a person to submit his or her will to a truth that contradicts their original opinion. In this case (really, in all cases), that truth is God's Word. As we do so, we figuratively bow our head to the authority of God, and we begin to think with the mind of Christ.

Sometimes people believe humility is being more self-deprecating. Sometimes people express false humility through jokes that belittle themselves. That's not humility. As C.S. Lewis wrote in *Mere Christianity*:

"Humility is not thinking less of yourself, it is thinking

of yourself less."[5]

This is the essence of humility. To, like Christ, possess great strength and still submit to the greater good of God's plan. Jesus demonstrated this during His struggle in the Garden of Gethsemane right before the Crucifixion. Jesus knew God's plan was the cross, and even though Jesus didn't want to follow the plan, He did. His tremendous humility in that moment made it possible for all of us to receive salvation and eternal life.

"…Father, all things are possible for You. Take this (crucifixion) away from Me; *nevertheless, not my will but Your will be done."*[6]

In spite of His inclination, in spite of passing thoughts of an easier way, Jesus *humbled* His mind before God the Father. As a result, all of mankind was given the opportunity to be rescued from death and Hell.

Follow Christ. Have a mind like Christ. *Be humble.*

Be Separate

Romans 12:2 gives further instruction on having a renewed mind, on making your mind more like the mind of Christ. Paul writes, "Do not be conformed to this world, *but be transformed by the renewing of your mind* that you may prove the good and acceptable and perfect will of God."

Once again, the renewal of the mind is connected to the will of God. In the first example, Christ's mind was humble enough to submit to God's will. In this verse, renewing your mind happens by avoiding conformation to the world; by separating your mind from the influence of the world that sets itself against the things of God.

Paul instructs the Corinthians (and all of us who read the New Testament) to, "Come out from among them, and be separate."[7] Fully understanding what it means to be in the world but not of the world is critical to the renewal of your mind.

Today's world is flooded by the tsunami of digital output streaming from TVs, computers, video games and speakers. Try going into any retail environment without being bombarded by sights and sounds, all designed to influence your thoughts and decisions.

Just the other day, while pumping gas into my car, a video screamed at me to join the latest rewards club. It is no exaggeration to say that there is no "off" switch in the digital age.

There is no end to the influences and inputs that stream relentlessly to our minds via speakers and screens. Each moment is packed with a message from someone trying to sell something. As a result, our minds become like a ping-pong table, with ideas bouncing around and around like a little white ball across our gray matter.

Now more than ever, we need to pause. We need to separate. We need to "take every thought captive"[8] by focusing on the Bible, the Holy Spirit and God's active presence in our daily life. The human mind's ability and tendency to wander is strong and nearly continual. So, how do we become separate in our thinking so that we may renew our minds?

Since turning off our thoughts completely is not an option, I recommend substitution. *Replace the thoughts of this world and your flesh with the thoughts of God.*

Here's a practical example to test yourself. What is the first thing you do when entering an empty car? An empty home? Is your first instinct to turn on the radio? The TV? Try silence for longer than a few minutes and see what happens.

I'm convinced that we often don't hear God's voice because we are drowning Him out. We blare music and TV and overwhelm the still, small voice of God. Pause. Listen. Be still and silent.

Once you've heard from God, continue renewing your mind by focusing on the things of God. What are the things of God?

Once again, the apostle Paul has provided a blueprint for accomplishing this. In Philippians 4:8-9, he teaches the church:

*Finally, brothers and sisters, whatever is **true,** whatever is **noble,** whatever is **right,** whatever is **pure,** whatever is **lovely,** whatever is **admirable** – if anything is **excellent** or **praiseworthy** – think about such things…and the God of peace will be with you.*

Put this list in front of you. Write it in your journal. Stick it on your car dashboard. This verse should remain wherever you need it to keep you mindful of the need to separate your thinking to the things of God.

Remember, as a man thinks in his heart, so is he.[9] The thoughts that you allow to invade your heart will make you. Or they will break you. Be separate. Renew your mind.

Be Persistent

Often, success is found through simple persistence. In business, in relationships, in athletic training, in every human competition, achievement comes – almost by default – by being the last man standing. The willingness of a person to persevere is the key attribute for any measure of achievement. Sometimes, it's the *only* thing necessary for achievement. In the case of Australian Olympian Steven Bradbury, being the last man standing won him and Australia its *first ever* Winter Olympics gold medal.

In 2002, at Salt Lake City, Bradbury was representing the Land Down Under for the fourth time in his career. He was a short track ice skater and a serious underdog, going against the likes of American legend Apolo Ohno. The short track ice skating race is an intense one, with tight quarters and bumping and shoving. Kinda like NASCAR, except without cars, and on ice.

In the final race, as he was rounding the last turn, he was in fourth place, hoping for some burst to at least win a bronze medal.

As he looked down the track, he got something far more unexpected. All three skaters ahead of him moved too close to one another. First one lost his balance, then another, and suddenly, all three were tangled up and crashed to the ice.

Before any of them could get back up and going, Steven Bradbury glided past them all and across the finish line. On the biggest day, in the biggest race of his life, Steven Bradbury won a gold medal, simply by being *the last man standing*. By being persistent.

Being persistent is critical in life, especially when it comes to renewing the mind. Few, if any, parts of God's creation are as unruly and cunning as the human mind. The potential for extraordinary good or incomprehensible evil exists within the human mind. As an example, all I have to do is type one famous and one infamous name from the past one hundred years:

Mother Teresa

Adolf Hitler

As you read those names, you immediately felt a reaction. The first name likely inspired admiration, joy, and a desire to be more charitable to your fellow man. The second name caused you to recoil in horror and even rage as you thought of the Holocaust and all the innocent people who were slaughtered by an evil man with an unrenewed mind.

What would people's reaction be to the mention of your name? Hopefully and likely, it's much closer to Mother Teresa. The ancient Greeks had an expression that works well in this context: **gnothi seatuon**, or **Know Yourself.**

In order to be persistent in the pursuit of renewing your mind, you must first "know yourself". That is, you must be honest and objective as you recognize the natural inclinations of your own mind. Each of us wages an internal battle every day. In our thought life, we face as much temptation from within as we do from the outside world.

Once you come to terms with your weaknesses, you will

be far more likely to tackle the daily work of renewing your mind.

Here are a few practical ways to be persistent and renew your mind:

1. Begin each day in prayer
2. Read the Bible
3. Listen to worship music
4. End each day in prayer

Your spiritual mind needs multiple opportunities through-out the day to successfully overcome all the natural thoughts that bombard it. Since your thoughts manifest themselves through your speech, review your conversations with this simple reminder from Eleanor Roosevelt:

Shallow minds discuss other people; Average minds discuss events; GREAT minds discuss ideas.

Be persistent in your daily devotions and prayer. Be consistent in your thoughts, using Philippians 4:8 as your guide. Reflect on your conversations to determine if you are truly renewing your mind. Be vigilant. Don't allow yourself to go on "auto-pilot". If you stay persistent, if you pursue the renewal of your mind wholeheartedly, you will discover that you can indeed have the mind of Christ.

Stay Humble – remember what Jesus did for you.

Stay Separate – make time to hear from God and to get away from the noise of the world.

Stay Persistent – faithfully follow God and focus on His words, His Spirit, and His plan for your life.

If you consistently follow these truths, you will renew your mind and have the mind of Christ. You will be well on your way to choosing life, blessing and prosperity for your life and your family.

Renew Your Heart

After a lengthy confession of his moral failings and God's power to save and forgive, King David declares in Psalm 51:10, "Create in me a *clean heart*, O God, and *renew* a steadfast spirit in me."

David, as much as any man, recognized the evil within his own heart. He understood this so much, he asked God repeatedly to, "Search me, O God, **and know my heart... see if there is any wicked way in me and lead me in the way everlasting**."[10]

David, the shepherd boy who defeated Goliath and earned the favor of King Saul and the adulation of the Israelites, knew that he wasn't always pure and he wasn't always the conquering hero. David, the youngest son of Jesse who was left in the field when the prophet Samuel came to anoint the next king, knew that his heart wasn't full of innocence.

Not long after his ascension to the throne, David discovered just how wicked and vile the human heart could be. One particularly wicked day, he was lazy and remained at home when he was supposed to be leading his men in battle.[11]

As he strolled along the rooftop of his castle, he noticed a beautiful woman across the way. Because David was not at war. He was idle and he was prone to impure thoughts about this attractive lady.

David sent a servant to find out who she was. The report came back that she was, "Bathsheba, the *wife of Uriah the Hittite*".[12]

As soon as David became aware of her marital status, he should have ended the desire for her that was percolating in his heart. But he was already predisposed to sin because he had allowed his heart to lead him to a place of idleness. And so, he continued…

He sent for Bathsheba. She arrived, as the King had summoned her. Soon after that, David took her and had sex with her. He committed adultery because he allowed his wicked heart to overrule the moral laws of God.

Perhaps he rationalized his behavior. Maybe he thought that no one would ever know. After all, Bathsheba's husband, Uriah was off at war. Uriah was fighting for Israel, as David should have been.

But, as God told the Israelites long before David was King, and as experience has taught us, "your sin will find you out."[13] Sure enough, David's sin found him out. A month or two passed and he received word from Bathsheba that she was pregnant. There's no getting out of it, either, because Uriah has been at war. David is the only one who could possibly have been the father. He didn't even need to go on the Maury Povich show for a "paternity DNA test reveal" episode to find out.

Now what? Does he confess and repent? Does he feel guilt and shame that he, as King of the entire nation, has taken a poor soldier's wife?

No.

He allows his heart to continue to devise wickedness. *You see, when you begin to weave a web of deceit, you usually end up tied up in the knots of your own lies and cover-ups.* This is exactly what happened to David. His first response was to send for Uriah.

Uriah returned from battle and David urged him to go to his house and "wash his feet"[14], an Old Testament-era euphemism for Uriah to go be with his wife. Instead, Uriah stayed near the door of the palace.

The next morning, David asked Uriah why he didn't go home. Obviously, David hoped that Uriah would sleep with Bathsheba, allowing David cover for his adultery.

Uriah replies, "The soldiers are encamped in the open fields (of battle). Shall I then go to my house to…lie with my wife? As the King lives, I will not do this thing."[15]

I can imagine David rolling his eyes at Uriah's dedication. I can also imagine David's heart pounding as he refuses to end his scheming. That night, David had Uriah eat dinner with him, and as they dined, David made sure Uriah became intoxicated. Now, David hoped, Uriah is drunk and will surely go home and sleep with Bathsheba!

Even the influence of alcohol was insufficient when it came to Uriah's loyalty to the traditions of war. He refused to enjoy his life and his wife while his counterparts were fighting and dying on the battlefield.

David was exasperated. Does he finally confess? No. He allowed his wicked heart to continue its reign of terror. He decided to simply remove Uriah from the equation. David sent Uriah back to war carrying a note, sealed by the King's ring. Uriah, as a good soldier, never opened it. He delivered the letter to Joab, the commanding officer, unaware that he had just carried his own death sentence to the army camp. Joab broke the seal and read the following instructions:

Set Uriah in the front of the fiercest part of the battle, and retreat from him that he may be struck down and die.[16]

Joab obeyed the command of the King, and Uriah was killed. David's wicked heart took him from a place of idle laziness to adultery to murder! I'm sure on the morning that David should have been at war, he couldn't have imagined that he'd find himself sending a great soldier into a place of guaranteed execution. Yet, this is the pull of the deceiving heart. It starts mild and ends up wild, ravaging and destroying others to protect itself.

David's example is vivid and valid. For one, David was not a "bad guy". It's easy for us to see someone like Charles Manson as evil and "not like us". Terrorists and serial killers are simply different. So, what about David? He committed adultery and murder. Yet, God declared of him, "I have found David, son of Jesse, a *man after my own heart...*"[17]

David was a man after God's heart. He was the chosen King of Israel. He wrote most of the book of Psalms. He loved God. The book of Acts tells us, "David served his own generation by the will of God, then fell asleep."[18] He was a remarkable man, used by God for remarkable purposes.

Yet even he was capable of horrific, heinous crimes.

If David needed to renew his heart, how much more do we?

Clearly, the Old Testament prophet Jeremiah was right when he wrote, "The heart is deceitful above all things and desperately wicked. Who can understand it?"[19]

By now, you should be convinced of the need to renew your heart. Don't worry, I didn't bring you this far to leave you without hope. You can renew your heart. You will renew your heart. Let's get started. Like any process, it's best to begin at the beginning:

Repent

Before we explore how David repented, I think it's important to renew the mind regarding repentance itself. Many people are burdened with guilt and shame and as a result, avoid repenting altogether.

Repentance is nothing more than "turning away" from going in the wrong direction in your life. The Bible encourages us to "be zealous"[20] to repent. In repentance, we stop the downward spiral of sin and we begin the rise to restoration and fulfillment of God's purposes for our lives. Think about it for a bit. Repentance is not a bad thing. It's a necessary thing. It's a healthy thing, and it will bring health to the broken places in your life.

Since I used David to demonstrate the pure wickedness found within the human heart, it's only fair to teach how we can renew the heart as David did. He's not mentioned here just to be a whipping boy – he became a true winner in the Kingdom of God. And it began when he truly repented.

After Uriah was killed, the Bible says, "Bathsheba mourned for him. After the time of mourning was over, David brought her to his house, and she became his wife and bore him a son. *But the thing David did displeased the Lord.*"[21]

God was upset. And He didn't waste any time telling David so. God sent Nathan, a prophet, to the King's palace. Nathan told King David a story about a rich man who took a poor man's only lamb. As Nathan told the story, he pretended that it was real and asked David for an answer as to what should be done about the rich man.

David "burned with anger"[22] after hearing Nathan. He said, "As surely as the Lord lives, the man who did this must die!"

Nathan replied, "You are the man. God says, I gave you everything – I protected you. I gave you the kingdom. I gave you all Israel and Judah. If this were not enough, I would have given you more. *Why did you despise the word of the Lord by doing evil?* …because by this deed you have given great occasion to the enemies of the Lord to blaspheme, the child also who is born to you shall surely die."[23]

The consequences of David's un-renewed heart were swift and severe. God brought disruption and death to David's kingdom. As Nathan spoke, David began the process of renewing his heart. He replied simply, "I have sinned against the Lord."

Renewing your heart begins with confession.

The act of confession is a foundational one in renewal of the heart. If we don't declare to God the things we have done wrong, He can't forgive us. He can't begin to renew our hearts.

1 John 1:9 tells us, "*If we confess our sins, He is faithful and just to forgive us our sins.*"

The use of the preposition "if" is important. It sets up a conditional statement. Since there is an "if" condition, there is also an "if not" alternative. His forgiveness is conditioned upon our confession. If we don't confess, He won't forgive. If He doesn't forgive, we will never have a renewed heart.

As David did in Psalm 51, a psalm attributed as his response to God after his adulterous and murderous actions, we must ask God's forgiveness for the wickedness in our hearts. The moment we begin to speak to Him, and truly repent of our sins, He begins to renew our heart.

We must also confess to one another. If your sin has wronged another, you must ask for their forgiveness. Sometimes, the sin we are holding onto actually causes physical symptoms.

Psalm 32:3-4 illustrates, "When I kept silent about my sin, my body wasted away...My vitality was drained as with the fever heat of summer."

James 5:16 says, "Confess your sins one to another and pray for one another, that you may be healed."

According to Dietrich Bonhoeffer, the act of confession brings us back to the cross of Jesus Christ.

Confession in the presence of another is the profoundest kind of humiliation. It hurts, it cuts us down, it is a dreadful blow to pride. In the confession of concrete sins the old man dies a painful, shameful death...Because this humiliation is so hard, we continually scheme to evade confessing to another (like David). *In confession we break through to the true fellowship of the Cross of Jesus Christ, in confession we affirm and accept our Cross.*[24]

Remember, this book is all about choosing life. Sometimes, choosing life will feel like death. But, what's dying is the old nature, the wicked heart. It is crucified like Christ through confession. Which is why confession is so difficult. It's why people will carry secret sins for decades and even generations. The fear of being shamed and scorned, as Jesus was on the cross, is powerful. It's a deception, however. The devil and our flesh know that the moment confession begins, true healing and renewal of the heart is underway.

It's important to know the Biblical pattern of confes-

sion. You aren't supposed to run around declaring your sins to everyone. Confession must be done, but it should be done properly and discreetly.

I experienced a unique situation with confession years ago when I was running a small group. One of the men in the group was a CFO from a major corporation. I'll call him Arthur. Arthur had been saved from alcoholism, found his place in church and served God with gladness.

One day, his wife shared with me that Arthur seemed to be acting differently. I observed him more closely during our next meeting and I too noticed that he was withdrawn and distant.

I asked him what was wrong. At first, he denied that anything was wrong. Later that week, he called me and said that he had been embezzling from his company. He had stolen tens of thousands of dollars. He was afraid to tell his wife, and he was rightly afraid of going to jail.

I told him that God forgave as soon as he repented, but that the right thing to do was to confess to his wife and to his employer.

Of course, just because someone confesses, doesn't mean they shouldn't be wise. Arthur got an attorney, after he confessed to his wife. The three of us went to his employer to tell the truth. To clear Arthur's conscience and to make things right.

I'll never forget the attorney's comment before we went to the meeting. After reviewing all the possible scenarios – from no charges and no jail time to fifteen years in prison – she leaned across the desk and told Arthur, "The hard part is over."

The hard part is over? I thought. *What about jail?*

She continued, "The hard part was bringing it into the light. Now, every day is one day closer to full restoration and redemption." We went into the enormous corporate office. I watched and listened as Arthur bravely confessed all. He had worked for this company for years. He was the Chief Financial Officer. Now he sat before the CEO and confessed his crime. His betrayal.

The CEO responded in a way I didn't expect. Although, when someone confesses of their own volition I often see mercy granted, that's not always the case. The CEO would have been within his rights to be punitive. Yet, he wasn't.

He looked at Arthur, who was trembling a bit. Who wouldn't be?

The CEO said, "We aren't going to press charges. We suspected this was going on. Of course, you can't have your old job, but we'd like for you to tell us how you did it so we can protect our company from embezzlement in the future."

Arthur's confession is very instructive. It should be done discreetly, and with pastoral assistance. But it should be done, sooner rather than later.

There is an interesting irony inherent in confession. Often, those who try to save face by hiding a sin or crime, ultimately lose face when their sin finds them out. Conversely, those who are willing to lose face to make things right often get a second chance and end up saving face because people respect those who are forthright about their failings.

As Jesus pointed out, "Whoever wants to save their life will lose it, but whoever loses their life for Me will find it."[25] Confession is part of losing your life for Christ's sake. It's denying pride and selfishness the power to control your life.

The next time you struggle with confessing your failings either to God or a fellow Christian, remember the power of the cross. It was in the act of surrender and humiliation that Jesus brought life to all. In the same way, when you confess, you bring true life and true renewal to your own heart.

Worship God

As David repented, he went from confession to worship. This is a common experience in the process of heart renewal. As a person finally uncovers and reveals his or her sins, the power of that sin to control him or her is broken. As sin's power is broken, the natural response is one of thanking God for His forgiveness. As freedom enters the heart, the same mouth that uttered dreadful deeds of sin through trembling lips begins to shout with joy with gratitude for God's redeeming work.

In Psalm 51, David demonstrates the transformation from confessor to singer of praises. Of course, David was a songwriter and a musician, but even if you don't sing except in the shower, you should follow his example.

After he spends the first half of Psalm 51 confessing his failures and asking for God's forgiveness, he says, "… open my lips, Lord, and my mouth will sing forth your praise."[26]

Shortly after that, he writes "…I trust in the mercy of God forever and ever. *I will praise You forever…*"[27]

Your heart will be renewed when you confess and repent. The joy that you receive through forgiveness from God and your fellow human will lead you to a spirit of gratitude and rejoicing. Take the time after repentance to worship God. You will feel the power of the Holy Spirit working in you, renewing your heart and giving you liberty to follow God into the future.

Pray in the Spirit

The baptism of the Holy Spirit is a significant and vital part of renewing the heart. More than that, it's a cornerstone of living for Jesus. If you have not yet received the baptism of the Spirit and you do not pray in tongues, contact your pastor to discuss and believe for this important part of your life as a Christian.

Also, read *Overdrive: Life led by the Holy Spirit*, a Wave Church publication, to gain a complete understanding of baptism in the Spirit.

King David did not have this New Testament blessing from God. So, in this regard, we have an advantage – a powerful advantage – over the mighty King David. We can pray in the Spirit, as the apostle Paul did. As the early church did, growing in faith and power as a result.

Praying in the Spirit edifies the inner man. It strengthens the heart. As you pray through the Holy Spirit, you are built up in your faith and your heart is renewed. Praying in the Holy Spirit, allowing the Spirit to pray through you leads to prayer that is the *will of God*.[28] A day shouldn't pass that a Spirit-filled Christian avoids this powerful and important activity.

Confess and repent for any sins that have prevented you from receiving God's forgiveness.

Worship God. Praise Him for the life He's given and the mercy He's shown you.

Pray in the Spirit. Daily allow the Holy Spirit to pray through you God's perfect will for your life.

Following these steps won't guarantee you have a "perfect" life, but they will renew your heart and lead you into God's best for yourself. By renewing your heart, God can use you in bigger and better ways and the world around you will be blessed through your life.

Renew Your Speech

Speech is powerful. Everything we experience on earth, even the earth itself, is a result of words. God's words, spoken in the beginning, created the world.
God created His world, and everything in it (including you and me), by speaking. "Let there be…"

The first chapter of Genesis explains that in the beginning, the earth was without form. It was void. Empty. The Spirit of God was hovering. It was waiting for God to speak. When God spoke, the Spirit of God and the Word of God worked together to create the world.

We are made in the image of God, and we create our "world", our future, with our words.

A less theological expression is as follows:
"Sticks and stones may break your bones, but words will bruise your soul and crush your self-esteem."

Wait a minute. That's not the way the old playground expression goes. But that's the truth. Your bones can be set and cuts will heal, but the scars caused by words last a long, long time and can ruin your life.

James writes, "Out of the same mouth comes blessing and cursing. My brothers and sisters, these things ought not be."[29]

The book of Proverbs, written by David's son Solomon, has much to say about the power of the tongue – for good and evil:

A soft answer stops wrath, but harsh words stir up anger.[30]

He that has knowledge spares the use of words.[31]

Death and life are in the power of the tongue...[32]

Remember, this book is about choices. It's about choosing life. The above verse makes it clear: if we are going to choose life, we must choose the right words. The words you use determine your direction. They influence your actions and the actions of others. **With your words, you choose life or death.**

When your body is sick, your words can reinforce the illness and give it power. Many times I've heard people say, "I don't feel well." Sure they don't – they just said it. What we say eventually comes to pass.

Everybody knows someone (or is that someone) who just can't seem to say anything positive. They grumble about everything and point out the negative in every situation. If the weather forecast calls for rain, they say, "I knew it." If the weather forecast calls for a beautiful sunny day, they say, "Oh, I'm sure the weatherman is wrong!"

No one wants to be around these people for very long. On the other hand, we all know someone (or are that someone) who speaks good things and positive reminders to our hearts. We all want to be around people like this. **A good way to guarantee that you can be around positive speaking people is to be one yourself!**

By our speech, we reveal our desires. By our speech, we express our dreams. Vitally important, a condition to salvation is confessing with our speech that He is Lord. Making God choices, having God desires and dreams requires renewing our speech.

Renewing our speech is as important as any of the other chapters in this book, but renewing our speech is dependent on the actions taken in response to Chapters 2 and 3, *Renewing Your Mind* and *Renewing Your Heart.*

Why? The Bible explains how integral the mind and the heart are to our speech:

*A fool utters all his **mind**, but a **wise man keeps his tongue…**[33]*

*A good man brings good things out of the good stored up in his heart, and an evil man brings evil things out of the evil stored up in his heart. **For the mouth speaks what the heart is full of.**[34]*

*Truly I tell you, if anyone **says** to this mountain, "Go, throw* *yourself into the sea," and...**believes that what they say will happen, it will be done for them.**[35]*

The first verse, and many others in Proverbs, reminds us that a wise person holds his or her tongue. They don't talk first, they think first. They know the power of words and so, they use them with discretion. It reminds me of what Abraham Lincoln said:

Better to be silent and thought a fool, than to open your mouth and remove all doubt.

That's a humorous quote but it illustrates what we've all experienced when we talk without thinking first.

Our words direct our energies. They determine our faith. A powerful illustration of this happened when the disciples were in a boat with Jesus. Matthew 8 tells us that a storm rose up, but Jesus was sleeping in the bottom of the boat. The fear-filled disciples, instead of trusting God, allowed their speech to give power to the storm.

Instead of declaring that God is bigger, God is greater than any storm and that He would save them, they screamed, "Lord, save us! We are going to die!"[36]

The disciples placed their faith in the storm, rather than God's power. Their speech revealed what they thought was most powerful – and it wasn't Jesus. It was the storm. Like the disciples, we often give power to the difficult times in our lives by talking about how bad things are, how we aren't going to make it, etc. How can we change this? By renewing our speech.

A renewed mind is essential to renewed speech. Remember Philippians 4:8? That's the passage that teaches the characteristics that should define our thoughts. *Noble things. Pure things. Beautiful things, etc.*

If your mind is focused on productive things and good things, your speech will reflect it. Renewing your speech is all about arresting your bad habits by cutting them off at the source. If you have a foul mouth or a negative speech pattern, you can stop it by thinking better.

Some people cloak their negative, death-producing language by saying, "I just speak my mind." As though everyone else is dishonest or withholding the truth. The reality is "speaking your mind" without renewing your mind is a recipe for disaster. **The next time you're tempted to spout off without analyzing a situation and applying the truth of God's Word to your thinking, hold your tongue. You'll be very glad you did.**

Jesus talked about a man's heart being good or evil. He said that what's in the heart will be revealed by speech. If you have a temper, if you have a lack of faith in your heart, if you have unforgiveness…you will be revealed by your speech.

On the other hand, if you have a renewed heart, your speech will bring good things like life, faith and healing to a situation. Proverbs 15:4 says, "A wholesome tongue is a tree of life..."

Wouldn't it be fantastic if everyone who knew you could say you had a "wholesome tongue"? How great would it be to use your speech to bring a tree of life wherever you go?

It's possible. ***With a renewed mind and a renewed heart, you can develop the discipline of renewed speech.***

Of course, this book is practical. Which means you're about to read some habits that you can form which will enable you to renew your speech. We are going to use the example of Paul to outline a few simple ways you can master the tongue. Speak Life. Speak Faith. Renew Your Speech.

Paul's Renewal

The apostle Paul was once named Saul. And Saul was not a good man. He did not have a renewed mind, though he was well educated. He did not have a renewed heart, though he was passionate and ambitious. He did not have renewed speech, as we will soon see.

The first time Saul is mentioned is in the book of Acts, chapter 7. This chapter tells the story of Stephen, who is considered to be the first Christian martyr. Stephen had a renewed mind, heart, and as Acts 7 shows, renewed speech. For fifty verses, Stephen tells the Pharisees who are about to kill him that Jesus was the Messiah.

He preaches to them, beginning with Abraham and ending with Jesus, about the nation of Israel and the wickedness done by men in the Pharisees role throughout the generations.

Stephen finishes by telling the Pharisees that they killed Jesus, the Son of God. They become irate. They can't wait any longer and they begin to stone him. Stephen has a vision of heaven and declares that he sees Jesus, "standing at the right hand of God."[37]

At the moment that Stephen is being killed, the Bible mentions, almost as an aside, "the witnesses laid their coats at the feet of a young man named Saul."[38]

Saul was training to be a Pharisee, in fact, he was the head of his class. He stood beside and watched Stephen killed without any remorse or regret. In fact, Acts 8:1 says, "And Saul approved of their killing him."

Saul's mind and heart had yet to be renewed. And his speech was no better. Acts 9:1-3 tells us, "***All this time Saul was breathing out murderous threats against the*** *followers of the Lord. He went to the high priest and asked for arrest warrants to take to Damascus, so that if he found any there who belonged to the Way, whether men or women, he might take them as prisoners to Jerusalem.*

Saul was cursing and declaring his intentions to murder Christians. Yet, as he started down the road to Damascus, fists full of authorization to arrest any followers of Jesus, God had a different plan. God was ready for Saul to renew his speech. God wanted Saul to change his language from death and blasphemy to faith and salvation.

God blasted Saul to the ground with a brilliant light from heaven. He blinded Saul and told him that He, "was Jesus, whom you are persecuting"[39]

God changed his name to Paul, and he went on to preach to the nations, and write most of the New Testament.

Paul couldn't refute what happened. He was radically saved. He had an experience few people have ever had – a direct, audible voice from heaven that gave him instructions for what he was to do. ***Even if your conversion didn't include a blinding light and a voice from the skies, you can still accomplish mighty works for God, just like Paul.***

Paul's speech was renewed. He went from speaking threats and curses against Christians to declaring in the synagogues that Jesus was the Messiah.

How did he do it? Here are three ways to renew your speech, based on the life and teaching of the apostle Paul:

Testify about Jesus

Notice that Paul immediately began telling people about Jesus. Of course, it's easy to think that it was easy for Paul. He literally heard from God. But, your conversion is no less real. No less important. Paul is no longer alive, so someone has to carry on the business of telling others about Jesus.

"At Iconium, Paul...went as usual into the synagogue. There he spoke so effectively that a great number of Jews and Greeks believed.[40]

When you begin to tell others about what Jesus has done in your life, your speech is pure. Even if it's not eloquent, it has power, because you are giving all the praise to God. As you tell about the great works of God in your life, your renewed speech will be a "tree of life" for everyone you encounter.

Notice that the verse above says that Paul "went as usual" into the synagogue, or church. Paul was intentional. He made a habit of going where people were gathered and shared the gospel. Make a habit of sharing the gospel with others. You don't (and probably shouldn't) have to go to a crowd and stand up and start yelling but you can plan to regularly testify about who Jesus is and what He is doing in your life. As you do, you'll find your speech reflecting the renewed mind and heart that you've already developed.

Be Gracious

In a letter to the Colossians, Paul gives an instruction that works well in the context of renewed speech. Specifically, he guides us in our speech to others, which according to experts, is about 150 words per minute, and is the bulk of our overall speech.

Since we talk to others daily, if not hourly, it's vital that our speech be renewed. **Every impression we make with our speech can draw people nearer to Jesus or repel them.**

Does your speech attract or repel?

Paul writes, "Be wise in the way you act toward outsiders; *make the most of every opportunity. **Be gracious in your speech. The goal is to bring out the best in others in a conversation, not put them down or cut them out.**"[41]*

Use your speech to invite others, to encourage others, to demonstrate the love of Christ toward others. Renew your speech by testifying about what Jesus has done in your life. Renew your speech by being gracious, even when others are rude. Finally, renew your speech by avoiding gossip.

Avoid Gossip

What is your first reaction when you sense the conversation moving to gossip? Do you engage and indulge the desire to trash someone (who isn't in the conversation) for his or her style, decisions, appearance, etc.?

Paul gave a tremendous amount of instruction to Timothy. In his first letter to his young protege, Paul warned about the dangers of gossip. He describes some of the people in the church as learning, "*to be idle, as they go around from house to house;* ***and not merely idle, but also gossips and busybodies, talking about things not proper to mention.*" [42]

It's interesting and instructive to see that the same behavior that led David to commit adultery also leads people to gossip. Idleness.

The word *idle* is defined as, "Not employed or busy; not active; **lacking purpose**."

When you lack purpose, it's easy to find a false sense

of purpose in gossip. It can feel like the conversation is addressing something that is wrong. Maybe it is even rationalized as a discussion about how to "help someone". **All gossip really does is demonstrate the gossiper's lack of purpose for his or her own life.**

Paul wrote to the Ephesians, "Let no unwholesome word proceed from your mouth, *but only such a word as is good for edification according to the need of the moment, that it may give <u>grace</u> to those who hear.*[43]

I've heard lots of excuses for gossip, but I don't think any qualify. Use Paul's instructions the next time you are tempted to gossip.

Is the speech good for edification? Does it give grace to those who hear? Does it give grace to the person being discussed? If not, avoid it like the plague. Tell people you're not interested in gossip. You want renewed speech, full of grace and encouragement.

Testify about Jesus. Tell others about His love and mercy. **Your speech will be renewed**.

Be Gracious. Show kindness. Use words of comfort and encouragement. **Your speech will be renewed**.

Avoid Gossip. Run from people who want to talk about others. Don't be idle. Have a purpose bigger than discussing what's wrong with others. Use only words that edify.

Your speech will be renewed.

Renew Your Environment

Every athlete who qualifies to participate as a swimmer for the United States goes to the same place to train. Colorado Springs, Colorado is home to the United States Olympic Complex and is headquarters for U.S. Swimming.

In 1997, the USOC officially opened a nearly $24 million facility, which included a sports science center, a sports medicine center, a dining hall and two residence halls, along with access to the multiple weight rooms, recovery rooms, swimming pools and other training aspects already in existence.

The reason that everyone on the team goes to the same place is simple. ***The right environment brings the best results.***

In Colorado, the swimmers train together, eat together, and live together. Everything they do is designed to reinforce and build their abilities to reach the maximum potential.

Imagine if the swimmers were just left to their own plans. Some might lack proper coaching. Others might lack the best nutrition. All would lack the most important element, working with like-minded athletes all pursuing the gold medal. **The first and most important factor for a**

right environment is a shared vision.

Likewise, Christians need the right environment to achieve the potential that God has placed inside them. Christians need not just a right environment; they need a **renewed environment.**

The environment we live in is corrupted. It has been ever since Satan deceived Adam and Eve. As a result, we struggle against the world, often in ways we don't see or understand.

As Paul told the Ephesians, "We wrestle not against flesh and blood but against principalities (fallen angels), against powers, against the rulers of darkness of this world, against spiritual wickedness in high places."[44]

Like the Olympic swimmers, we face temptations of laziness, fatigue, indulgence and apathy. The difference is our victory is much greater than a medal and a national anthem. Our victory is found in choosing life, literally. And our victory is much more assured when we put ourselves in a renewed environment.

A renewed environment is the final piece of the renewal process that leads to choosing life. A renewed environment cements the power of daily decisions that will create your God-desired destiny.

Before joining the swim team in Colorado, all the athletes

have trained and built their bodies into the right position and health to even qualify for the team. In a similar way, renewing your mind, heart and speech has qualified you to participate in a renewed environment. The mind, heart and speech are all dependent on your work with God. A renewed environment is dependent on your work and leadership among others.

It's clear that Christians need a renewed environment. What does a renewed environment look like? How can we find one? How can we create one? It begins by being a part of God's house.

The primary renewed environment for a Christian is the local church.

Actively Attend Church

The following excerpt from my book, *The Christian Walk*, explains the unmistakable importance of the local church:

The local church is a community of believers. Jesus command-ed that Christians "forsake not gathering together" to worship and learn more about God. God declared that the church is His strategy for Christians to work together, to support one another and to build His plan on earth until He returns.

Bill Hybels, pastor of Willow Creek Community Church,

says, "**The church is the hope of the world.**" I agree completely.

God instituted the church to be the one thing that nothing can stop…The Bible promises that those who are regular and active in church will have a life that grows and improves.

Psalm 92:13 says, "Those who are planted in the House of the Lord will flourish."

Planting implies depth. It suggests rootedness. It is imperative that you not only attend church but that you become truly rooted in a soul-winning local church.[45]

Joining and serving in a life-giving, Spirit-filled, local church is the first and most important step to creating and being part of a renewed environment. The local church is your God-ordained environment. It sets you up to go out into the world.

Being planted in church is kind of like the swimmers turning their head for air before submerging again to move forward through the water.

Every time you're in church, you get that breath of air, the inspiration of God that gives you the strength to go "underwater" in the world where you work and live. If you try to go too long without attending church, it's just like trying to swim underwater for too long. Eventually, you'll pass out. You might even die. It's not a risk worth taking.

None of the swimmers would even consider taking a second stroke in the water without gulping more oxygen. That oxygen is vital for the muscles in the swimmer's body to perform at full strength.

Likewise, no Christian should go a week without the life-giving power of church. As Hebrews 10:25 explains, we should "not forsake the assembling of ourselves (Christians) together…"

Every moment in the renewed environment of church brings more energy and faith for the spiritual muscles that will help you keep your renewed mind, renewed heart and renewed speech.

Set Healthy Boundaries

Even in the right environment, the swimmers could still fail to do their best if they don't stay focused on their goals. Daily reminders and checklists help each swimmer to stay on track and avoid the temptation to break the rules – the rules that are designed to carry them to the gold medal platform.

Even in a renewed environment, the Christian can still fail if he or she doesn't set healthy boundaries. Going to church isn't enough. A Christian needs daily reminders and scheduled time with God and like-minded believers if he or she is going to avoid the temptations that seek to derail him or her from making it to the best in God.

Unlike the training center, the church is a place that accepts everyone. The USOC training center is a place for elite athletes. Unless you're one of the best athletes in the world, access is denied. The church is the opposite of that. All are welcome. It's a place for ordinary sinners. In other words, it's a place for you and me.

Because of this reality, which is God's plan, there is a need for healthy boundaries. God commands us to love all and to share the good news of Jesus Christ with any who will listen. He does not command us to get sucked into the problems or sins the person is dealing with. **You can love and accept someone where they are without absorbing their troubles.** Often, I see new Christians enter the renewed environment of the church. They are excited and in love with everything that Jesus has done for them.

As the initial excitement wanes, they can go one of two ways. They can become disillusioned, when they realize the church is full of people who aren't perfect. Or they can become discipled, and continue growing and flourishing in God.

Discipleship, or receiving mentoring and teaching in small group settings, is the way to develop healthy boundaries in the church. For single men and women, this includes specific rules for dating. Regardless of a person's past dating behavior, which has been forgiven *and forgotten* by God, the path forward in dating relationships needs to be clearly marked. Like the swimmer's lanes are defined by floating plastic tubing, the Christian's relationships need to have clearly defined boundaries. Swim in the lane God has prepared for you.

Some simple steps for healthy boundaries in dating are as follows:

1. **Establish accountability** with a pastor or church leader. Be honest and open about your feelings, desires and intentions.
2. **Get involved in a small group**. Learn and develop an understanding of the discipline that Jesus wants you to follow.
3. **Have a vision for a clean, healthy life**. Without a vision, people die. With a vision, people choose life.
4. **Avoid late night dates in isolation**. "Nothing good happens after midnight" is not just an expression. It's a reality.
5. **Build friendships first**. New Christians especially need time to grow in Jesus. Adding a layer of dating will cause unnecessary limitations in walking with God. Trust God to bring the right person into your life.

As for general friendships, be wise in all relationships. Seek friendships with people whose life inspires you to seek God. Build relationships with people who are involved in church. With people who have a renewed mind and heart, as evidenced by their speech.

Don't allow everyone to know about your business. Choose a few close mentors to open up to. Protect yourself and remember the power of the tongue. Don't repeat bad news about others.

Set and keep healthy boundaries. Stay in your "lane" and you'll go fast and true to the destiny God has for you.

Follow God's Will

Many times people ask me about God's will, as though it is a specific set of actions. The popular conception is that God has a unique path for everyone to follow. The myth of God's will is that it can be easily missed because it is narrow and specific. While it's true that the path with Christ is "narrow and few there be that find it,"[46] I don't believe God's will is narrow. I discuss this in much greater detail in my book, *The Accent of Leadership,* but I'd like to share the following two points to keep in mind when thinking about God's will:

-   **God's Will is unfolding**

- **God's Will is for us to bear fruit**

God's will is unfolding. By this I mean that it appears slowly over time. In Colossians 1:9, Paul writes, "Since the day we heard it, we do not cease to pray for you and to ask that *you may be filled with* **the knowledge of His will in all wisdom and spiritual understanding.**"

God reveals His will in an ongoing fashion, which is why Paul said, "we do not cease to pray". Daily request from God the wisdom and spiritual understanding to be in God's will. Living in a renewed environment will position you to hear from God and follow His will.

God's will is for us to bear fruit. In Colossians 1:10, Paul explains that God's will is to, "walk worthy of the Lord… *being fruitful in every good work…* "

If you are being fruitful, that is, over time your efforts yield improvement and growth for your own faith, and bless the lives of others, you are in God's will. No matter what your vocation, being fruitful is a clear demonstration of a life in God's will. And since we already learned that those who are planted in church will be fruitful, the renewed environment once again provides the place to discover God's will.

Actively attend church. Stick with a local body of believers in a life-giving, Spirit-filled church. Be planted. Serve. Give. Love one another. The local church is the hope of the world, and it's the best renewed environment on Earth.

Set Healthy Boundaries. Avoid negativity. Work with a couple of mentors who inspire you to serve and pursue God. If you are single, use wisdom in dating. Avoid tempting situations. Serve in the church. The healthy boundaries of a renewed environment will help you win your race and "stay in your lane".

Follow God's Will. Stay patient. God will share details on a need-to-know basis. Trust Him. Bear fruit. Stay planted and grow and over time, you will see incredible results in your life and the lives of many others.

Renew Your Mind.
Renew Your Heart.
Renew Your Speech.
Renew Your Environment.

It's your Choice. Choose Life. Choose Right and watch your daily decisions give you a dynamic destiny!

(Endnotes)

Chapter 1

1   Matthew 27:22

2   Durant, Will: The Story of Civilization: Caesar and Christ. Pp. 557

3   Luke 15:10

Chapter 2

4   Philippians 2:6-11

5   Lewis, C.S.: Mere Christianity, 1952.

6   Mark 14:36

7   2 Corinthians 6:17

8   2 Corinthians 10:5

9   Proverbs 23:7

Chapter 3

10   Psalm 139:23

11   2 Samuel 11

12   2 Samuel 11:3b

13   Numbers 32:23b

14   2 Samuel 11:8

15   2 Samuel 11:11

Chapter 4

35	Mark 11:23
36	Matthew 8:25
37	Acts 7:56
38	Acts 7:58
39	Acts 9:5
40	Acts 14:1
41	Colossians 4:5-6
42	1 Timothy 5:13
43	Ephesians 4:29

Chapter 5

44	Ephesians 6:12
45	Kelly, Steve: The Christian Walk: Seven Steps to Living for Jesus, pp. 47-48
46	Matthew 7:14

About the Author

Steve Kelly is the Senior Pastor of Wave Church, a Christian church with national and international influence. Wave Church's two main campuses are in Virginia Beach, Virginia. It has multi-site campuses located throughout the state of Virginia, as well as North Carolina, with more to come.

Pastor Steve's passion is to win the lost and to lead the generations to find their purpose in Christ, through the building of the local church. Wave Church's primary mission is to help people do life well and find their purpose in Christ through being planted in the local church.

Made in the USA
Columbia, SC
18 May 2021

38170306R10037